Classic Cocktails

KUDOS

Published by Kudos, an imprint of Top That! Publishing plc.
Copyright © 2003 Top That! Publishing plc,
Tide Mill Way, Woodbridge, Suffolk, IP12 IAP.
www.kudosbooks.com

Kudos is a Trademark of Top That! Publishing plc

Introduction

The history of the cocktail is somewhat blurred. All that can be said for certain is that mixed drinks, both alcoholic and non-alcoholic have been drunk throughout the world for hundreds of years

Predictably, claims for the origin of the word 'cocktail' are accompanied by colourful and outlandish anecdotes. A popular story is that of Betsy Flanagan, an innkeeper during the American War of Independence. She is said to have served American and French officers a meal of roast chicken, stolen from a nearby English farmer. The officers washed down their meal with drinks decorated with the bird's tail feathers, mocking their enemy with toasts of "vive le cocktail!"

Another story tells of an American bar, where a large ceramic container in the shape of a cockerel was used to store the leftovers of drinks. The potent, if sometimes unpalatable mixture, was served from a

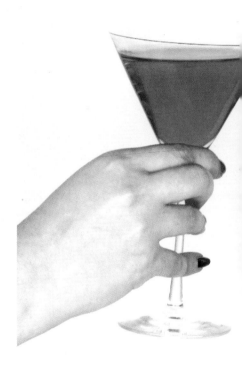

tap at the 'tail' of the bird, hence the term 'cocktail'. Other theories are based upon anything from drunken fighting cocks to docked horse's tails — every cocktail aficionado will have their favourite story.

The Martini is generally agreed to be the first modern cocktail. The classic mix of gin and vermouth, garnished with a cherry or olive was popular across the USA by 1900. However mixed drinks really took off during prohibition in the USA. The illegal hooch produced by the bootleggers generally tasted awful, so recipes were concocted to make it more palatable. Cocktail favourites such as the Harvey Wallbanger and the Manhattan all date from this time.

The classic cocktail conjures up images of style and sophistication, cool and glamour. Exotic-tasting mixes remind us of holidays, frivolity, fun and even danger. So try the recipes in this book and realise your own cocktail fantasy!

 page three

Equipment

**Making quality cocktails requires a
range of special bar equipment.
The cocktail shaker is essential.
Your need for the other items will
depend on the type of drinks you
make the most and whether or not
you are a stickler for detail**

Bar spoon

Long-handled spoons used mainly for
mixing drinks directly in the glass.
Also used for 'muddling' — crushing
sugar, herbs or other ingredients

Blender

Used for blending frothy cocktails or
mixing in crushed ice. The tall, goblet
style blenders are best for cocktails

Cocktail shaker

The three-piece shaker has a base to hold
ice and a built-in strainer. The larger
Boston shaker can mix drinks more quickly,
but you will need a separate strainer

Corkscrew/bottle opener
No bar would be complete without this

Fruit squeezer
Freshly-squeezed fruit juices are essential for certain cocktails

Measures
These are essential for measuring the right amount of alcohol — single (25 ml) or double (50 ml) shots

Mixing glass
A large glass beaker used to stir cocktails

Nutmeg grater
Does exactly what it says. Grates nutmeg very finely to top off Eggnogs and other frothy drinks

Strainer
Used with a Boston shaker to separate the pips and fruit pulp from the drink

Ice crusher
Used for crushing ice. Specialist mechanical and electric ice crushers are also available

Glasses

Good presentation is very much a part of enjoying cocktails. For some, only the correct glass will do, but you should use whatever you think looks good

(1) Champagne glass
The old-fashioned bowl is a very elegant and stylish way to serve Champagne or Champagne cocktails. However, the flute helps to preserve the fizz

(2) Highball/Collins glass
Tall tumblers used to serve long, ice-filled drinks with soda or fruit juice. The Collins is slightly larger than the highball

(3) Cocktail/Martini glass
This is the classic symbol of cocktail culture. Elegant, cool and sophisticated, the conical bowl on a tall stem is traditionally used for Martinis

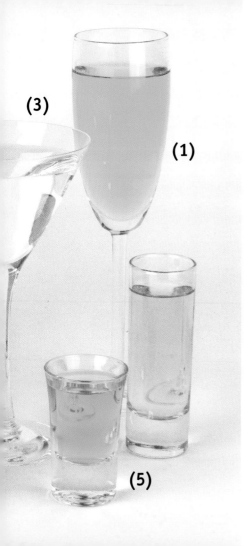

(3)

(1)

(4) Tumbler/rocks glass
Short, sturdy glasses used for serving
drinks over ice, or 'on the rocks'

(5) Shot glass
Very small glass used for consuming
(or measuring) shots of spirit

(6) Wine glasses
Various sizes are useful for wine and
different types of cocktails. Long stems
help to keep warm hands away from
your chilled drink

(5)

Techniques

Crushing ice

Many cocktails use crushed ice or 'ice snow' as an ingredient. You must crush ice before using it in a blender

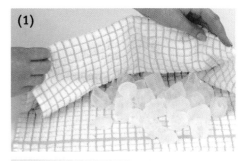

(1) Place a tea towel on a worktop and partly cover it with ice cubes. Fold the cloth over the cubes

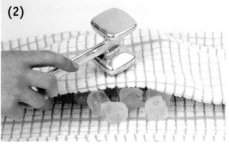

(2) Using a hammer, hit the ice firmly to crush it

(3) Spoon the ice pieces into your glasses or mixing jug. Large pieces can be stored in bags in the freezer, but the fine 'ice snow' must be used immediately

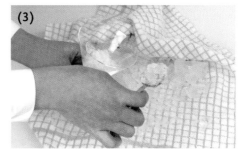

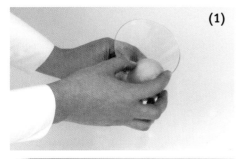

(1)

(2)

(3)

Frosted glasses

Many types of cocktails are enhanced by being served in a glass with a frosted rim. Salt or sugar are typically used, but you could create your own

(1) Holding the glass upside-down, rub the rim with the cut surface of lemon, orange or other suitable fruit

(2) Dip the rim in a shallow layer of the sugar or salt. Make sure the rim is well coated

(3) Leave the glass upright until the rim is dry. Chill in the fridge if necessary

Essentials and Tips

Flavourings
Essential cocktail flavourings include Tabasco sauce, Worcestershire sauce and Angostura bitters

Garnishes
Colourful and tasty garnishes can really make a difference to a cocktail. They should be fresh and of good quality. Cherries, lemons, limes and pineapples are common for sweet drinks; drier tastes may be finished with olives, celery or onions

Glasses
Make sure glasses are washed, dried and very clean. Never serve a cocktail in a warm glass — chill it in the fridge if necessary

Ice
Do not be afraid to use lots of ice. It keeps the drink cooler for a lot longer

Measures

An extra-large measure of alcohol does not improve a cocktail. Keep to the amounts shown in the recipes for reasons of class and authenticity. If you need more alcohol, mix up another cocktail!

Mixers

Always use the best mixers that you can afford. For juices, fresh is definitely best and make sure creams are not past their best. Some essential mixers include: cranberry, lemon, orange, lime, tomato and pineapple juices, cola and tonic water

Sweeteners

Fine caster sugar mixes into drinks well or even better make, or buy, some sugar syrup

Twist or slice?

A twist is a small strip of lemon or lime peel. Squeezing the twist over the drink will release the oils from the peel. Do not make slices too thick or thin

Contents

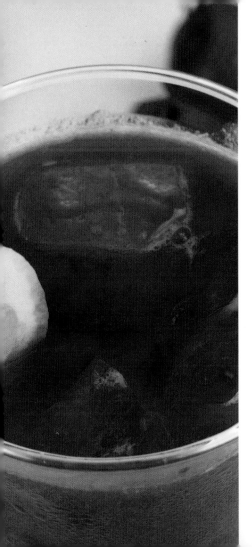

Applesinthe

Glass: Highball

Ingredients:
37.5 ml absinthe
Half a teaspoon of gomme syrup
One teaspoon of passion syrup
25 ml fresh lemon juice
12.5 ml apple schnapps
50 ml fresh apple juice
Dash of orange bitters

Method:
Shake ingredients and strain over crushed ice into a highball

Garnish:
With slices or wedges of apple

B-52

Glass: Tumbler

Ingredients:
15 ml chocolate liqueur
15 ml irish cream
15 ml cognac-based orange liqueur

Method:
Shake the ingredients together and pour over ice into a tumbler glass

Between the Sheets

Glass: Cocktail

Ingredients:
25 ml brandy
25 ml orange liqueur
25 ml white rum
15 ml fresh lemon juice

Method:
Shake ingredients with ice and strain into
a chilled cocktail glass

Garnish:
With a long lemon zest twist

Black Russian*

Glass: Tumbler

Ingredients:
50 ml vodka
25 ml chocolate liqueur

Method:
Pour the ingredients over ice into a
tumbler glass

Garnish:
With cherries

*You can turn the Black Russian into a
Long Black Russian by changing the
glass to a highball and topping
the drink with cola*

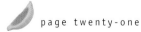

Black Velvet

Glass: Wine

Ingredients:
Champagne
Irish stout

Method:
Half fill a wine glass with the Irish stout
and top up with Champagne

Blood & Sand

Glass: Cocktail

Ingredients:
35 ml Scotch whisky
30 ml cherry liqueur
30 ml sweet vermouth
30 ml fresh orange juice

Method:
Shake ingredients with ice and strain into a chilled cocktail glass

Garnish:
With an orange slice

Bloody Mary

Glass: Highball

Ingredients:
50 ml vodka
180 ml tomato juice
Freshly squeezed juice of a lemon
Pinch of salt and pepper
One to three dashes of Tabasco sauce
Half a teaspoon of horseradish
Four to six dashes of Worcestershire sauce
Pinch of celery salt

Method:
Shake all the ingredients together with a scoop of ice

Garnish:
Serve in a highball glass garnished with a lemon slice and a stick of celery

Blue Hawaiian

Glass: Wine

Ingredients:
50 ml white rum
25 ml blue curaçao
100 ml pineapple juice
50 ml cream of coconut
Crushed ice

Method:
Add ingredients to a blender and mix for 20–30 seconds, pour into a wine glass

Garnish:
With a pineapple wedge and a cocktail umbrella

Bucks Fizz*

Glass: Flute

Ingredients:
50–100 ml freshly-squeezed orange juice
Champagne

Method:
Pour the orange juice into a flute and top
with chilled dry Champagne

Also known as the Mimosa

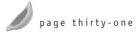

Caipirinha

Glass: Tumbler

Ingredients:
50 ml cachaca
One lime
Two brown sugar cubes

Method:
Cut the lime into eights and place into a tumbler glass with the sugar cubes and swirl together. Fill the glass with crushed ice and top with cachaca and stir

Garnish:
With a wedge of lime

Champagne Cocktail*

Glass: Flute

Ingredients:
25 ml brandy
One white sugar cube
Angostura bitters
Champagne

Method:
Cover the sugar cube in Angostura bitters
and place into a flute. Add the brandy and
top with Champagne

*This Cocktail is also known as the Classic
Champagne Cocktail and sometimes the
Business Brace*

Cosmopolitan

Glass: Cocktail

Ingredients:
50 ml lemon vodka
25 ml orange liqueur
Dash of cranberry juice
Squeeze of fresh lime

Method:
Shake and strain into a chilled cocktail glass

Garnish:
With flamed lime zest

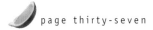

Daiquiri (original)

Glass: Highball

Ingredients:
50 ml golden rum
12.5 ml fresh lime juice
12.5 ml sugar syrup

Method:
Shake with ice and strain into a
highball glass over fresh ice

Garnish:
With a twisted slice of lime or serve in a
sugar frosted glass

Eggnog

Glass: Tumbler

Ingredients:
30 ml brandy
30 ml dark rum
One egg white
One teaspoon of sugar
Milk
Nutmeg

Method:
Shake all ingredients (except milk) with ice. Strain into a tumbler glass. Top up with milk

Garnish:
With a sprinkle of nutmeg

Fuzzy Navel

Glass: Tumbler

Ingredients:
50 ml peach schnapps
Orange juice

Method:
Pour the peach schnapps over ice. Top up with orange juice

Garnish:
With an orange slice

Gimlet

Glass: Cocktail

Ingredients:
50 ml gin
25 ml lime cordial
One lime wedge

Method:
Pour gin and lime cordial into a shaker with ice, squeeze in the lime juice and add the wedge. Shake and strain into a cocktail glass

Garnish:
With a slice of lime and a cherry or served in a frosted cocktail glass

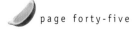

Grasshopper

Glass: Cocktail

Ingredients:
25 ml white crème de cacao
25 ml green crème de menthe
25 ml fresh cream

Method:
Shake ingredients vigorously and strain
into a cocktail glass

Garnish:
With cherries and a sprig of mint

Harvey Wallbanger

Glass: Highball

Ingredients:
50 ml vodka
12.5 ml galliano
Fresh orange juice

Method:
Into a highball filled with ice, pour the vodka and orange juice. Then float the galliano on the top

Garnish:
With an orange slice

Hawaiian

Glass: Cocktail

Ingredients:
50 ml gin
12.5 ml triple sec
12.5 ml pineapple juice

Method:
Shake all the ingredients together with some crushed ice. Strain and pour

Garnish:
With cherries and an orange slice

Income Tax

Glass: Tumbler

Ingredients:
50 ml of gin
12.5 ml of dry vermouth
25 ml of orange juice
Two or three dashes of bitters

Method:
Shake all the ingredients with the crushed ice. Strain and pour over fresh ice

Garnish:
With a slice of orange

Jamaican Slammer

Glass: Shot

Ingredients:
12.5 ml golden rum
12.5 ml triple sec
12.5 ml dark rum
Five drops of lime

Method: Pour the dark rum into the shot glass. Next float the triple sec and then add the lime juice before floating the golden rum on top

John Collins

Glass: Highball

Ingredients:
50 ml whisky
25 ml lemon juice
Dash of sugar syrup
Soda water

Method:
Shake the whisky, lemon juice and sugar syrup along with crushed ice. Strain and pour over more ice. Top up with soda water and stir gently

Garnish:
With orange and lemon segments and a cherry

Kir Royale

Glass: Flute

Ingredients:
10 ml crème de cassis
Champagne

Method:
Pour the cassis into a flute and top with
chilled Champagne

Long Island Iced Tea

Glass: Highball

Ingredients:
12.5 ml vodka
12.5 ml gin
12.5 ml white rum
12.5 ml tequila
12.5 ml triple sec
25 ml fresh lemon juice
Dash of gomme syrup
Cola

Method:
Build ingredients over ice into a highball glass, top with cola

Garnish:
With a slice of lime

Mai Tai

Glass: Highball

Ingredients:
50 ml rum
12.5 ml orange curaçao
12.5 ml apricot brandy
12.5 ml fresh lime juice
12.5 ml pineapple juice
Dash of Angostura bitters
Two dashes of orgeat syrup

Method:
Shake all ingredients with ice and strain
into an ice-filled highball glass

Garnish:
With a twist of orange

Manhattan

Glass: Cocktail

Ingredients:
50 ml whisky
25 ml sweet vermouth
Dash of bitters
A cherry to garnish

Method:
Stir together with ice, strain into a cocktail glass

Garnish:
With a cherry

Margarita

Glass: Cocktail

Ingredients:
25 ml gold tequila
25 ml triple sec
25 ml fresh lime juice

Method:
Frost the rim of the glass with salt.
Shake all the ingredients with cracked ice.
Strain and pour into the salt frosted glass

Martini (dry)

Glass: Cocktail

Ingredients:
50 ml gin
12.5 ml dry vermouth
Green olives or lemon zest

Method:
Pre-chill your glass, fill the mixing jug
with ice, add the pre-chilled ingredients in
the required ratios. Stir quickly and
smoothly for approximately ten seconds
and then pour into the chilled glass

Garnish:
Serve with olives or a strip of
lemon zest

Metropolitan

Glass: Cocktail

Ingredients:
50 ml brandy
25 ml sweet vermouth
A dash of Angostura bitters

Method:
Coat the glass with the Angostura bitters.
Shake the brandy and vermouth with
cracked ice. Strain and pour into a chilled
cocktail glass

Garnish:
With a cherry

Mojito

Glass: Highball

Ingredients:
50 ml light rum
Four white cane sugar cubes
(or dash of gomme syrup)
Seven or eight fresh mint leaves
A sliced and diced lime
Soda water

Method:
Muddle the mint, sugar and lime in a highball, then fill the glass with crushed ice, pour the rum, top up with soda and stir

Garnish:
With a sprig of mint and twist of lime

Moscow Mule

Glass: Highball

Ingredients:
50 ml vodka
25 ml fresh lime
Ginger beer

Method:
Build ingredients over ice into a
highball glass

Garnish:
With a wedge of lime

Nelson's Blood

Glass: Flute

Ingredients:
25 ml ruby port
Champagne

Method:
Pour ingredients into a champagne flute

October Revolution

Glass: Highball

Ingredients:
50 ml vodka
50 ml coffee liqueur
50 ml crème de cacau
50 ml double cream

Method:
Shake ingredients with ice, strain into a
highball glass containing ice

Garnish:
Serve with a straw

Pina Colada

Glass: Highball

Ingredients:
50 ml golden rum
25 ml cream
25 ml coconut milk
50 ml pineapple juice

Method:
Shake ingredients with ice and strain over
ice into a highball glass

Garnish:
With a pineapple wedge and a cocktail
umbrella

Pink Gin

Glass: Tumbler

Ingredients:
50 ml gin
Dash of Angostura bitters

Method:
Pour ingredients over ice into a tumbler
glass and stir to chill

Garnish:
Squeeze in oils from a lemon zest and use
a slice of lemon as garnish

Pink Lady*

Glass: Cocktail

Ingredients:
25 ml gin
25 ml orange liqueur
25 ml fresh lemon juice
Dash of egg white (optional)
Dash of grenadine

Method:
Shake ingredients with ice and strain into a chilled cocktail glass

To change into a White Lady take out the dash of Grenadine

Red, White & Blue

Glass: Shot

Ingredients:
12.5 ml grenadine
12.5 ml peach schnapps
12.5 ml blue curaçao

Method:
Pour the grenadine. Next float the peach schnapps, then the blue curaçao

This cocktail works better if you chill the ingredients beforehand

Rob Roy

Glass: Cocktail

Ingredients:
40 ml Scotch whisky
25 ml sweet vermouth
A dash of Angostura bitters

Method:
Add ingredients to an ice-filled mixing glass and stir until chilled. Strain into a cocktail glass

Garnish:
Garnish with lemon zest and a cherry

Make a 'Dry Rob Roy' by replacing the sweet vermouth with a dry vermouth and make a perfect Rob Roy by using half sweet and half dry vermouths

Rusty Nail

Glass: Tumbler

Ingredients:
30 ml whisky
30 ml drambuie

Method:
Pour ingredients over ice into a
tumbler glass

Garnish:
With a slice of orange

Sea Breeze

Glass: Highball

Ingredients:
50 ml vodka
150 ml cranberry juice
50 ml grapefruit juice

Method:
Build over ice into a highball glass

Garnish:
With a lime slice

Sex on the Beach

Glass: Highball

Ingredients:
25 ml vodka
25 ml peach schnapps
200 ml fresh cranberry juice
100 ml orange juice

Method:
Shake ingredients with ice and strain into a highball filled with fresh ice

Garnish:
With orange or lime slices

Singapore Sling

Glass: Tumbler

Ingredients:
50 ml gin
25 ml cherry brandy
5 ml sugar syrup
15 ml fresh lime juice
Soda water

Method:
Shake ingredients with ice and pour
into a tumbler glass filled with ice.
Top with soda water

Garnish:
With a slice of lime

Thin Blue Line

Glass: Shot

Ingredients:
12.5 ml of triple sec
12.5 ml of vodka
Four or five drops of blue curaçao

Method:
Pour the triple sec and float the vodka
carefully over the top of it. Then, with a
straw or dropper, add the curaçao drops

*This cocktail works better if you chill the
ingredients beforehand*

Tokyo Silver Fizz

Glass: Highball

Ingredients:
25 ml vodka
25 ml melon liqueur
12.5 ml lemon juice
Dash of egg white
Soda water

Method:
Shake ingredients (except soda) and strain over fresh ice into a highball. Top with soda water

Garnish:
Top with a lemon slice

Vodkatini

Glass: Cocktail

Ingredients:
50 ml vodka
A dash of dry vermouth

Method:
Stir the vermouth and vodka with ice in a
pre-chilled mixing glass. Stir until chilled
and strain into a frozen cocktail glass

Garnish:
With a pitted olive or lemon zest

Whisky Sour

Glass: Tumbler

Ingredients:
50 ml of whisky
25 ml of lemon juice
25 ml of sugar syrup

Method:
Mix the ingredients in a tumbler glass over ice

Garnish:
With a twist of lemon

White Russian

Glass: Tumbler

Ingredients:
50 ml vodka
25 ml chocolate liqueur
25 ml single cream

Method:
Pour vodka and the chocolate liqueur into a tumbler glass filled with ice. Layer the cream on top

Garnish:
With a stemmed cherry

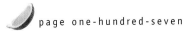

Xantippe

Glass: Cocktail

Ingredients:
50 ml vodka
25 ml yellow chartreuse
25 ml cherry brandy

Method:
Stir the ingredients vigorously with ice.
Strain into a chilled cocktail glass

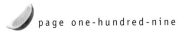

Yellow Ribbon

Glass: Tumbler

Ingredients:
50 ml mandarin vodka
20 ml lemon juice
10 ml frangelico
10 ml gomme sugar syrup

Method:
Shake and strain into a tumbler glass

Garnish:
With a lemon wedge

Zombie

Glass: Highball

Ingredients:
25 ml lemon juice
2 teaspoons of grenadine
2 dashes of Angostura bitters
25 ml spiced rum
200 ml orange juice
25 ml apricot brandy
100 ml guava/mango/other exotic juices
25 ml light rum
12.5 ml 'float' of dark rum

Method:
In a highball glass pour the ingredients
in order as above

Garnish:
With lemon and lime slices

Non-alcoholic cocktails

Non-alcoholic cocktails allow drivers, teetotallers and children to join in with the fun spirit of a cocktail without the obvious side effects that the alcoholic versions have

Often vibrantly fruity and refreshing, and with equally exotic mixes of ingredients, you'll hardly notice the difference as you sample the delights of a Brown Horny Toad, a Honeymoon or maybe a Starburst, that can be enjoyed any time of day, in any situation

Brown Horny Toad

Glass: Highball

50 ml pineapple juice
50 ml orange juice
25 ml lemon juice
5 ml grenadine
5 ml gomme syrup
Pinch of ground cinnamon
Pinch of ground cloves

Method:
Shake ingredients with ice and strain over fresh ice into a highball

Garnish:
With an orange and lemon slice

Caribbean Cocktail

Glass: Tumbler

Ingredients:
Fresh mango (peeled)
A banana
Juice of an orange
A dash of fresh lime juice

Method:
Blend the mango and banana with the juices and a few ice cubes until smooth. Strain over fresh ice into a tumbler

Garnish:
With slices of banana and a cocktail umbrella

Honeymoon

Glass: Cocktail

Ingredients:
25 ml clear honey
12.5 ml fresh lime juice
25 ml orange juice
25 ml apple juice

Method:
Shake ingredients with crushed ice and
strain into a cocktail glass

Garnish:
With a cherry

San Francisco

Glass: Wine

Ingredients:
25 ml fresh orange juice
25 ml fresh lemon juice
25 ml fresh pineapple juice
25 ml fresh grapefruit juice
12.5 ml grenadine
A dash of egg white
Soda water

Method:
Shake ingredients (apart from soda)
with ice and strain over fresh ice into a
wine glass and top up with soda water

Garnish:
With lemon, lime and orange slices

Starburst

Glass: Highball

Ingredients:
1 banana
1 kiwi
10 fresh strawberries
150 ml apple juice
Crushed ice

Method:
Slice fruit and place into a blender
with apple juice. After blending pour into
a highball

Garnish:
With strawberries

Glossary

All of the ingredients needed to make
the cocktails in this book are listed

Absinthe
*Infamous, very powerful spirit. Said to have
hallucinogenic properties*

Angostura bitters
Bitter flavouring derived from tree bark

Apple juice

Apple schnapps

Apricot brandy

Banana

Blackcurrant vodka
Vodka with a twist of blackcurrant

Blue curaçao
Liqueur flavoured with orange peel

Brandy

Cachaca
White Brazilian rum made from sugar cane

Celery

Celery salt

Champagne

Cherries

Cherry brandy

Chocolate dust
Powdered chocolate for garnishing

Coconut cream

Coffee liqueur

Cognac-based orange liqueur

Cola

Cranberry juice

Cream
Single and double

Cream of coconut

Crème de cacao
Brandy-based cream liqueur with cacao

Crème de cassis
Brandy-based cream liqueur with cherries

Crème de menthe
Brandy-based cream liqueur with mint

Dark rum

Drambuie
Whisky flavoured with honey and herbs

Eggs

Frangelico
Hazelnut liqueur

Gin

Ginger beer

Golden rum

Gomme syrup

Grapefruit juice

Green olives

Grenadine
Syrup derived from pomegranates

Ground cinnamon

Ground cloves

Guava juice

Horseradish

Ice

Irish stout

Kiwi

Lemon juice

Lemons

Lemon vodka
Vodka with a twist of lemon

Light rum

Lime juice

Limes

Mandarin vodka	**Rum-based coffee liqueur**
Vodka with a twist of orange	**Salt**
Mango	**Soda water**
Mango juice	**Spiced rum**
Maraschino cherries	**Sugar cubes**
Melon liqueur	*Brown and white*
Milk	**Tabasco sauce**
Mint leaves	**Tequila**
Nutmeg	**Tomato juice**
Orange bitters	**Triple sec**
Orange curaçao	*Sweet, white curaçao*
Orange juice	**Vermouth dry**
Orange liqueur	**Vermouth sweet**
Oranges	**Vodka**
Passion syrup	**Whisky**
Peach schnapps	*Irish, Scotch and Rye*
Pepper	**Worcestershire sauce**
Pineapple	**Yellow chartreuse**
Pineapple juice	*Liqueur flavoured with orange and myrtle*
Ruby Port	